MW01175127

Another Forty Years

Mike Nelson

Cover Photo by Thomas Cooper
www.lightboximages.com

Cover and book design by Nancy Bush,
Violette Graphics & Printing

ISBN 978-1-4675-8973-4

Published by

Senile Monk Press

South Berwick, Maine

A very special Thank you to John-Michael Albert for spending many hours with me performing orthographical surgery on this book. And for his many years of friendship and mentorship. He's made me a better thinker and a better writer. For all that I am deeply grateful.

"Mike Nelson and I have been friends since he first appeared on the New Hampshire Seacoast poetry scene in 2005. He was one of the first members of our poetry work-shopping group, Blood on the Floor. Mike is a member of the impressive generation of forty-something, blue-collar fathers who are successfully balancing career and home life with artistic expression. Since his first book, The One in the Middle (2005) and the following chapbook, Sometimes at Night (2007), fans of Mike's have been waiting for a compendium of the strong poems they have been hearing at open mic venues throughout the Seacoast. Another Forty Years (2013) is that book. Mike has created a "New and Selected" that includes old favorites like "The Barn Door," "Hole in the Wall" and "Meader Pond," and new works that range across his sense of humor ("Book Review," "Pee on the Bee") rapturous narratives ("Don't Touch the Frogs," "Picking Blueberries at Sturgeons Cove"), divorce and dating ("Divorce," "Of Man"), and metaphysical musings ("I finally understand," "The Mouse"). In the classic lyric tradition, Mike draws on nature as his chief source of inspiration and consolation, and his audience and readers are rewarded ten-fold every time."

John-Michael Albert
8th Portsmouth, New Hampshire Poet Laureate

~~~~~~~~~~~~

"Another Forty Years is a book torn out of Mike Nelson's own wild and beautiful soul. These poems are meant to be savored many times - heard, felt, tasted - in order to tease out the complicated nuances of humor, joy and bittersweet relationships contained in each lovingly crafted word. They move easily between a mystic spiritual worldview to the smallest mundane detail of being fully and completely alive. Mike is a gifted spoken word artist; listen to him speak the poems and then read them all over again for yet another inspiring sensory experience."

Genevieve Aichele
Artistic Director, New Hampshire Theatre Project

"Mike is an incredible poet and performer. His imagery is so vivid, honest and alive that we cannot help but follow him wherever he wishes to take us; we are in a relationship which has become a battlefield the instant the arrows are loosed, we hear the footsteps coming up the stairs of an old farmhouse and feel the scream stuck in our throats, we are witnessing the experience of loss and the inner-workings of soul through a lens of nature and myth, and sometimes we are just laughing our asses off."

Mara Flynn
Actress, Musician and Director of Acting Out
Newburyport, Massachusetts

~~~~~~~~~~~

"Mike writes with such honesty and heartfelt emotion that I begin to look at everything around me differently. His poems are filled with insight, pathos and humor. Here is a thoughtfulness that resonates a long time after you stop reading."

Lindsey Coombs
Poet

for Sofia
dansar i köket

Contents

Angie (1989)

Your boyfriend and my girlfriend
went off in a limo together
to a *Violent Femmes* concert;
and across our coffee and pink-frosted doughnuts,
we looked at each other,
perplexed.

So you made a call from a pay phone,
and we left the Hudson *Dunkin' Donuts*,
got into my metallic blue 79 Firebird,
drove to Woody's house,
bought a dime bag,
found a dead-end tractor path into a field,
turned off the car, except for the tape deck,
and smoked.

All I remember after that is
pure giggles.
Your eyes sparkling in the dashboard lights,
your endless toothy smile,
strains of *Roger Waters* from behind *The Wall*,
and the most genuine fun I'd had in seventeen years.

I don't remember what time it was
when I drove you home but,
when you opened the car door to get out,
I grabbed your hand,
because high school was over.
Our respective relationships were just about over.
Life as we knew it was over.
And I said, "Thanks, Angie."

In the milky, muted glow of the car's interior light,
in the otherwise total darkness of your mother's driveway —
the darkness of the whole world —
we hugged.

That's all I needed to know —
although, twenty-five years later,
I know it more now, than I ever could then,
what a real friend you were.

Inequities

As much as you expect it
you will never scare me away.

Your own prophecy fulfilled —
eyes narrow,
my treaty in shreds,
blowing away on the wind behind you —
you wait for the attack.

But I just stand there, quiet.

You call for the catapults to be loaded,
for arrows to be dipped in fire and drawn.

But I just stand there, quiet.

Believing all the awful things
you ever heard about yourself,
you raise your sword and slash the air,
shaking, screaming,

    FIRE!

You stare across the field into the whites of my eyes;
and in the brief silence of all projectiles aloft,
you hear me say,

I love you.

The Barn Door

I awake to a sound outside,
creep to the window to see.

The barn door was flung open by the wind
and now repeatedly swings open and shut—
Slam! Slam!—again and again.

I wonder if the horse is okay.
Should I check?

The wind will die down soon.
The barn door slams again.

Suddenly, I hear another door slam.
This time it comes from downstairs.

No one else is home.
They haven't been for years.
The nearest neighbor lives a mile away.

I shoot a look at the clock.
The power is out.

Fear is released from my primal base
and runs, breathless, up my spine.

The wind blows.
The barn door slams.

Heavy footsteps move across the floor downstairs,
slowly.

The door from the kitchen into the hallway
creaks open.

Footsteps move.

The kitchen door slams.
The barn door slams.

Footsteps are now at the bottom of the stairs,
ascending the stairs.

With each fall of a footstep
the barn door slams.

The footsteps reach the top of the stairs.
Just outside my bedroom door — they stop.

All four valves of my heart
slam in rhythmic unison with the barn door.

I jump deep beneath the covers of my bed.
The bedroom doorknob jiggles; the door creaks open.

Footsteps enter my room
and stop at the foot of my bed.

The sound of heavy breathing permeates the room.
The barn door slams.

Against my will, slowly,
I drop the covers to see what horrifying fate awaits me.

And what I see at the foot of my bed is...
THE HORSE! —

motionless, staring at me,
with a crazed bloodshot look in his eyes that says...

"Could You Please Fix The Barn Door!
I CAN'T SLEEP!"

Book Review

It doesn't matter what I say. I just want the review to say,

"He's so good,
I didn't know what happened until three days later
when I woke up in Mexico face down in the mud
with the words *SING THIS* tattooed on my ass."

I want the review to say,

"I opened the book and there was a knife and a feather,
and the word, *CHOOSE*. So I arrogantly chose the feather.
And a giant hawk came down, clutched me in her talons
and took me to her nest where she fed me to her young
and I was pumped through their innocent hearts
as they flew for the first time."

I want the review to say,

"This is so dumb and stupid that it's amazing."

because a good review makes intelligent people
feel like they're missing something.

The review should put the poems in a box
and use serrated words to saw them in half —
not like a magic trick; but like a sacrifice,
the blood draining into goblets
while doves are released
and trumpets herald the dawn of a new age in writing.

"Hear Ye! Hear Ye! Look! Oh My God! More Poems!
You need this book on your shelf! It will look so good
crammed in there next to all the other books.
Important trees are being cut down, as we speak, to make more.
Earth laid to waste while aliens invade to harvest our inspired brains.

"Oh, yeah! These poems are THAT FUCKING GOOD!"

Boozy

In the shadow of this tree
only the stars
and Boozy, the night owl cat,
can see me.

Long shards of neglected neighbor porch light
lay broken in the grass.

My apartment is right there but,
like Boozy,
I need to be out,
to be without.

Dormant swing.
The child sleeps,
dreaming of you.
But the sound of crickets rides high
in the stillness of your seat.

Air alive with chant,
jumping off the swing,
up, up, over the tree,
through all the scientific layers—
the borealis quilt of dreams—
into the luminous numinous.
Can't stop it.

"Yeah, Boozy.
Now's a good time to yowl.
Set it free, you crazy cat!"

Wait

But what if we stayed
while giving love its space?
Nature has no door but death
and we are still here,
so all dreams must include us.

My bee hums in the low flowers,
your bird proclaims in the high tree,
and the wind moves us both,
carrying our songs to each other's ears.

Who would we have been without each other?
Indeed, who will we be?
The earth keeps her secrets,
in hidden, wooded pools
beneath thick screens of algae,
in the muck of rotted leaves:

spores sprout tendrils
in the diffuse, undisturbed light,
grow towards the blue air
to become pad, to become lily
to become the resting place of a frog.

The Day After Goodbye

The house is quiet.

But the phone is quieter.

The house pops
and even thuds once in a while,
like an exclamation point
or a question mark on the silence.

But the phone offers no reply,
no sign of life.
Of course it is only a messenger;
but how I'd love to kill it.

The house gives a knock
like a comma, asking for more.

I stare at the phone: nothing.
Its eyes, and ears, and mouth are shut.

The Devil Walks into a Bar

Things had been bad for a while.
They were toiling with each other
long before I got to know them.
In fact,
the whole bit about what went down in Eden?
She planned it.
She didn't want to talk to *him* anymore.
She felt trapped. She wanted out, man.

But why, you may ask,
would she implicate herself, take credit
for Original Sin and The Fall and everything?
Because, *fuck him*, that's why.
That arrogant prick always going on about
being the first one, how *she* was made from *him*—
which was *bullshit*. I was there, man.
Some guys will say anything
to assuage their own meaninglessness.
I mean, what a lunatic. She'd had enough.

So, she asked me if I'd help,
you know, if I'd go along with it.
I said, "Sure baby, you know me.
I'm always up for some trouble."
And of course it worked out 'cause
I got my own vendettas. I mean,
there's only ever been one skin
I've been trying to get under.
And she wasn't thinking small;
she was going strait to the top.

But Big G did what Big G always does:
smiles and all of nature shook and wept
like teenaged girls at a Beatles concert.
And I just rolled my eyes.

You know,
anything anyone ever said that Big G said
was either a lie or wrong.
The only one anyone ever talked to was me.
They just didn't know it.
Well, some of them knew it.
Yeah, I put on a pretty good show.

Although, lately, times are tough.
It's hard to get peoples attention.
Everyone's so saturated with destruction
they're just not surprised or even bothered
when it happens. But it's not just that.
It doesn't matter what disguise I wear,
some people see right through it
and they'll just smile, like Big G does.
It's like people are starting to realize
it wasn't Big G who closed the garden,
but other people, people who wanted
to keep all that fruit for themselves.
And once your fear of God is gone,
the gate is wide open.

Which leads me to another thing
you've been misled about.
I wasn't kicked out of heaven
and banished here. I was sent here,
to light little fires under all your asses
so you wouldn't fall asleep.

Yeah, but like I said, these days are tough
and I find myself listening more,
especially to women.
I've always loved women.
They're so much more honest with themselves,
and they've paid for it—just like me.

Divorce

It was not like Humpty Dumpty; unless
it was the Wailing Wall he was sitting on,
and the kings horses and men where those apocalyptic four,
not there to pick up the pieces
but with trumpets blaring,
heralding the fall.

And it was not like Gone With the Wind; because
I have tried and, frankly, my dear,
it is impossible,
while everything is going up in flames,
not to give a damn.

And it was not at all like Lord of the Rings; unless
Frodo got frustrated and quit,
just gave the ring to Faramir in Henneth Annun and
went sulking all the way back to his hobbit hole.

Is there any story
with such an inglorious ending?

No mythos, but cold paper to be signed.
No climax, but mounting debt.
No heroes, but the one I imagined myself to be.
No victory, but humility.

Maybe it was like Genesis,
but Adam left the garden alone.
And after he cast a sideways glance
at those God-blinded cherubs
and that whirling, flashing sword,
he turned his eyes forward,
barely concealing a smile; because
in the darkness between his tunic and skin,
stolen with his tongue from the mouth of Eve,
the apple's seed.

Don't Touch the Frogs

My maternal grandfather died
when I was eleven.
He was a giant, Italian man
who loved sausage, yard sales
and betting on the horses.

My parents, my two brothers and I
got on a plane to Florida
to clean out his trailer near the Everglades.
There were half a dozen blenders
with price tags still on them.
The freezer was full of pizza and kielbasa.
And my mother found a wad of cash
in every pair of pants she picked up.

Our father told us, "Don't touch the frogs."
They weren't like the ones back in New Hampshire.
The Florida frogs were everywhere,
bright luminous greens and yellows,
with stripes and spots.

I would get as close to them as I could.
They were less real and more fantastic the closer I got.
They would sit there, daring me to touch them;
and I had to keep reminding myself not to.

Driving away from the trailer that evening,
I saw a thunderstorm in the distance.
The lightening bolts were so numerous, so concentrated,
it looked like a giant, otherworldly jellyfish
lumbering across the plain
in a floating ocean of its own making.

Next day, I slipped, hit my head on the edge
of the hotel swimming pool and fell into the water.
There was nobody there but my younger brother.
If not for him I am sure I would have drowned.

That night, in the hotel room I shared with my sleeping brothers,
I turned on the TV in the middle of The Exorcist.
I watched Linda Blair's bed dance in mad circles,
while someone in the room beside ours
stumbled into furniture and slid chairs across the floor.

I was far away from home
and my parents were far away within themselves.
I knew that Disney World was somewhere nearby.
I wanted to go there to make this reality a fantasy:

to plunge, forgotten, into the noisy darkness
of Mr. Toad's Wild Ride;

to strap myself into that runaway train for a mad roll
down Thunder Mountain;

to come up for air in the briar patch
on Splash Mountain;

to taste the bitter trials of innocence
in Snow Whites Scary Adventures.

**Family Vacation,
or How I Survived an Oxymoron**

Where the hell are we?
Where the fuck is the spatula?
Is all this chipped paint supposed to be charming?
And what is that smell?
Why did we do this to ourselves?

All the people I've worked so hard to avoid
are here, in the same house,
on one of the most beautiful stretches
of rocky-coasted ocean in the world —
with nothing to do.

There are children here.
Nothing is more antithetical to rest and relaxation
than children.

What? No television?
Whose twisted Rockwellian vision of togetherness is this?
Cans of beans and freeze-dried coffee?
Was there a nuclear war that someone forgot to tell me about?

And did you see that bar of soap in the bathroom?
It is fused to the porcelain by its own decomposing goo —
and it has a hair on it!

What? You're bored? We just got here.
We're going to be here for a week, you know.
You what? You want me to play with you?

Oh, my God, I have to get out of here.
Where are the keys?
I don't care if I have to drive a hundred miles to find one —
I'm going to *Dunkin' Donuts*!

The Fire

What will become of this earth,
our eternal bed?
Shall we lie here forever
in sexual Samadhi,
yoga of love,
drawing lines between the stars,
tracing our history through
one glorious annihilation after another?

It's all shifting beneath us,
because of us,
fear's seismic erosion,
salt dust of angels on our tongues.

The fire that has been used by gods and men
to scorch all things holy
is the same light that halos us,
making our vulnerability beautiful.

We are the moment to be found
and these flowers are the trumpets,
growing around us, over us,
bringing the bees,
heralding with gold dust and bumble
a new world.

First Snow

What was it like then?
Neanderthal's of Eden
Sticking out their tongues.

Me, Tarzan

Forget Adam and Eve;
I grew up thinking Tarzan, Jane and Boy
were the first humans.

Every time I visited my grandfather's apartment
I imagined a chair flying through the air.
My mother told me
that her parents threw furniture when they argued.
I could picture my mother in the next room,
scared, crouching under the table.
My mother and grandfather would talk in the kitchen
while I sat on my grandfather's bed
and watched Tarzan on his little black-and-white TV.

Tarzan was always nice to Jane.
I couldn't imagine them throwing furniture at each other;
and I couldn't imagine Boy having to hide from them.

From my grandfather's bed,
I felt angry when other people
invaded Tarzan and Jane's jungle Eden.
I wanted to see an episode
where they swung from vine to vine
beneath the glittering canopy,
bathed in waterfalls,
and ate bananas and drank coconut milk
as they watched the sun set
from their treetop home;
and Boy played with tigers,
swam with crocodiles,
giggled at pythons,
and slept peacefully every night,
cuddled next to Cheetah on a giant branch.

The jungle echoed with Tarzan's call for help
on the TV. I could hear my mother and grandfather
laugh in the kitchen.

The Glass Wall

I know you're there. I can see you;
but this pane has grown thick.

Where did it start? A secret resentment,
like a spider from the heart
spinning a gossamer lattice
to catch our diminishing light.
But subtle treasons
become treaties of silence,
and the spider keeps spinning
until web becomes wall.

Without our shared myth,
we begin to make up stories of our own.
Like Gollum, alone in the mountain,
we fret and fracture over The Precious,
the promise, the rings on our fingers
that have made us invisible to each other.

And we wail at the wall,
stuffing notes into the cracks;
but no one reads them.
There we rock, back and forth,
like disturbed, forgotten children.

Does anyone remember what all this was for?
Can you tell me? Do you know?

I hear you tapping on the other side of the wall,
our eyes re-engage through the glass.
The spider retreats.
Ten thousand shards crash to the floor.

The Goodbye Theory

Because it wasn't okay to be yourself,
how birdsong was imprisoned.

That spanking and then dead god of childhood,
like all other gods mistaken for god,
was more like a salamander with a severed tail.
So you learned the way of the severed tail,
to hide in wet, uncomfortable holes.

We like to say "the universe this" and
"the universe that" to let ourselves off the hook;
but love knows too well your resigned face.

That background distortion is the dirge
of a mourning prayer or laughter in the hallway.
Both want you to listen, to join in, to say goodbye—
how birdsong is sprung.

Hole in the Wall

I started at five in the twilight of dawn
long before I was awake.
But the factory was always on
twenty-four hours, seven days a week.
Myself and about seventy, mostly Asian, women,
stood in two long rows facing a conveyor,
all in hairnets, caught like dolphins,
placing fish sticks in boxes, still dreaming, unawares.

Out of a giant square hole in the wall
the fish sticks poured through,
from the ocean they were hauled.
Once synchronistic and mysterious schools,
beheaded, shredded, breaded, fried and frozen.
Our minds, like our fingertips, turning numb,
place and time, forgetting where and when,
hopes and dreams whitewashed by the factory drum.

Could this be the hell of which I've been told?
What loves have I forsaken to arrive at this end?
All these others and I funneled through a similar hole
like that one through which our labor is sent.
But, of course, we chose this,
ours and the world's worth already denied.
Will not one of them look up and notice,
join my prayer in a communion of eyes?

But my hands begin to lose their pace;
boxes need to be filled.
Lesser thoughts swim into place;
mind resumes its mechanical will.
But, betraying this, I see a tear fall.
I look up from the conveyor's motion:
through the hole in the wall
I hear the sound of the ocean.

Form

I am the shadow by which the day remembers me,
not the body, but the song that greeted us when we came.
You are the forest where hunger came of age.

And this pang of desire—how evening reaches for morning,
this scripture of geography, this dialect of mimicry—
written with my fingers in braille upon your skin,
as we both go blind,
feeling our way through the undecided country of night.

Of Man

I borrow her voice
when my eyes refuse to speak,
but then my hand folds into hers
and that lets my eyes off the hook.

She thinks I'm strong;
but doesn't she notice me
trying to burrow inside her?
And when I point that out,
she thinks I'm even stronger.

Woman is the calendar wanting to be filled.
Man is the lost pen.
And God is asleep at the kitchen table,
face down in the mash potatoes.

I tell her I'm afraid. She smiles and hugs me.

Doesn't she see that winter is coming
and that all these windows are broken?
Doesn't she see that I've built no fence
for those horses outside?

She laughs and I kiss her fast.
My madness strikes against hers
and we ignite, engulfed in flame.

The next morning, our bodies in a tangled heap,
eyes open to birdsong. She smiles at me again.

I give up.

Three Problems

I finally understand,
which is not to say there is no room,
for other's final understandings.

And this disclaimer must be stated.

There are those who will see the words
"I" and "finally" and "understand"
and will not read this
without such a disclaimer.

There are others who will also not read this
because it *has* a disclaimer,
but not as many.

At this point if you are still reading or listening,
then it is you who I would like to talk to
and we can forget about the others —
for now.

As I said, I finally understand;
but now I see how that word "finally" is a problem
because it has come up so many times before,
so let's drop it.

I understand something. It is very difficult to say.
Many have tried before; I feel I must try now.

This understanding is alive,
and these words, all words,
are feathers falling from the sky;
and the understanding is over there now,
singing in a tree.

Is that what I'm trying to say?
I'm not sure that's it.
Not much of an understanding, I guess,
so let's drop that word as well.

Which leaves us with "I"
which has always been a problem.
Not the gift it keeps trying to think it is
but really just a box full of feathers.

So let's drop the "I" as well.
Open the box. Let the wind in.

Now maybe the others will come back,
and I can apologize to you all
for wasting your time.

Savor

I have seen your heart,
the light breaking through the slats,
the dome half-built over a mountain,
the abandoned tools.

I remember the mud rinsing off your legs,
puddling around your feet,
the scratched skin that I kissed
the taste of what I wished were true.

We switch off all the lamps.
Trees get the hint.
Roots hum beneath the earth,
the language we tried to learn

Words that failed us,
and gave way to tears:
all the salt
that kept us preserved.

The Woolgatherer

I just saw the rest of my life
pass before my eyes.
An angel.
No, an archangel.
Maybe an archetype.
Maybe she was me.
Who's to know?
I don't know.
But all I know
she was spaghetti and meatballs,
my favorite movie,
Sunday with nothing to do.
And we could do all that and more
together,
true love forever.
That is
if I had just talked to her.
But I didn't
and she's gone.
But wait,
here comes another,
the rest of my life.
What a goddess.
She's a Renoir in the boudoir.
She's a sunset in Spain
with a glass of wine.
She's so fine.
She could be everything.

Oh man, here she comes.

And there she goes.

Outside the Gate

I wish you were next to me
at the edge of this field
so I could say goodbye,
because I've had enough of missing you.

Soon I'll be walking
straight into this surging ocean of wildflowers
to drown in waves of yarrow and milk vetch,
to let aster and goldenrod fill my lungs,
to sink into chicory and milkweed.

I wish you would come with me,
hold my hand as we leap into the prairie dock
and hoary vervain,
die with me in the ironweed and lavender,
make halos of pearly everlastings,
let angel spiders spin our gossamer wings.

I wish you were next to me
at the edge of this.

Expanse

If you worry about floating away,
I will worry about being heavy enough to hold you down;
and if I imagine I'm coming up short,
you will wish that you could shrink to my size.

The sidewalk is just like that safe margin we write ourselves into,
avoiding the risk of listening,
the words that turn our quiet moments into questions,
the fasting that thins the veil and sets us adrift in the hunger of
holiness.

The cow in the field says more than I:
Holstein inkblot grazes next to the neuron tree
as crows re-uptake too quickly into the sky.
We'll call it "getting ahead of ourselves."
The crows excrete undigested seeds;
one might fall into the cow dung and take root there.

This is how the earth was covered with flowers.
This is how the earth was covered with everything.
It took along time; let's take our time.

The Masturbation Poem

If there is only one thing I've learned in life,
it's that one should always masturbate outside.

Masturbation is making love to whatever's around you,
and when I'm inside, love is halted by the walls.
The smaller the room, the smaller the pleasure.
Dead linear structure and fixtures
share not one of my breaths.
They are all bored or asleep.

But outside there is no stopping it. Trees shake.
Grass prickles like hairs on top of goose bumps.
Flowers forsake the bee and turn towards me.
While clouds move aside so the voyeur sun can stare.

Best of all is at night,
hidden by darkness in plain sight,
and not just one seeing star
but billions and billions of twinkling eyes.

Light not just from far away
but from far a-when,
too long to be counted by moons.

Here, man may stroke the root of reason and history
and find all his holdings limp,
woman may plumb the depths of love
and find only her ever aching void.

Here, inadequacy and frustration
become blameless and equal,
what is released
is not reflected or reciprocated but keeps going
far beyond the reach of the hope of our needs,
all the way out and back,
to the beginning and past it
and past the end before that.

Will you join me anyway in the night garden,
splayed out on our backs,
the tops of our heads almost touching,
with crickets leaping over our exhibition,
I with a slow grip, you with lazy fingertip circles
and warm orgasms of laughter
taking flight above us.

In Between

You drove all the way across the country
with the radio off.
It was America's silence you needed to hear,
preamble of corn fields, purple mountains, rivers
and the highway between your old life and the new one,
a dream that needed your lucid attention.

Not all the country music, but the music of the country.

Chasing the sunset through endless amber waves,
beneath a sky growing bigger and bigger
was waking up to a truth that laid buried
your whole life in the noise of change,
now bristling in a gathering storm on the western wind.

Contract

In the dark meadow the snake sleeps,
our Adam and Eve forget all about God
and say what they really think,
because darkness makes them feel invisible.

Remember staying up late in the tent?
Beyond the veil of nylon there was nothing
but the ghost of wind.
The only light in the universe was our flashlight.
When held under our chins, it turned our faces ghastly,
like all the monsters we imagined were lurking outside.
After that, with pinkies locked,
we told each other things that never left the tent.

Whispering in the grass, love is found, felt and forgotten,
like civilizations, like us, making love with words,
not wanting it to end — but it always does.
Every moment truly felt is bittersweet.
I love, love this feeling of not knowing where it's all going.

Wait. Did you hear that?
Quick. Pull the sleeping bag over our heads.
Take my pinky in yours
and tell me your secret before we get eaten alive.

In the World

When you said I wasn't "in the world" enough
I scoffed and accused you of not being "in yourself."
But later, as always, I regretted what I said
and wondered what we really meant.

Instead of these abstractions,
like "the world" and "the self,"
let's call it "the moment."
Let's ask, "Are either one of us in it?"

To be born is to go searching for something.
But we get lost in the world, and in ourselves,
in the old definitions of each.

But what did we find in each other?
In that first look, that transcended both "world" and "self,"
we remembered something.
We want to call it "love,"
but let's call that "the moment" too.
Again, let's ask, "Are we in it?"

In those times of utter nakedness,
clothes strewn about like ripped-out pages of a dictionary,
we stopped, looked into each other's eyes,
and the world and ourselves and love became indistinguishable.

We were not searching anymore.
Not dying anymore.
Not being born.
Something inside us grew
and the world grew with it.

Inside My Coat

Inside my coat
a faux flock of geese are heading south,
away from hard decisions,
from all the bittersweet break-ups
of trees and leaves,

and you are somewhere,
rustling beneath that pile,
carving premature angels
into my affected season.

Inside my coat is nothing
but a stuffing for the crows
and the masked and disfigured children at the door
holding out their bags for more.

Inside my coat
I am falling like the darkness
between equinox and solstice,
shivering and deficient behind this thin veil of science.

How often I have betrayed you for warmer times
when only T-shirts or even less were required,
when bikini tops replaced bras
and everyone felt free beneath sky's dimpling blue cheek.

But, in the sound of arms moving through these sleeves,
a lie is whispered inside my coat,
as some ghost in the wind
swipes my hand from the zipper.

Inside my coat
polyester-down dreams of this lake
that will soon be ice,
and we may walk across,
hand in hand,
like I tried to do alone last summer.

Inside my coat
spring returns too soon,
and the mud remembers
a single footprint, now filling with water
where a bird takes a bath
inside my coat.

Long Distance

I was going to say something about the chicken I cooked:
six boneless chunks in olive oil and garlic,
enough for two.

But then your friend's friend talked about
living on his boat in Grenada
and the whole other world beneath it that he scuba dived in.

I was going to say something about
how I wished you were in bed with me
so I could read you this long Li-Young Lee poem,
which was really just one poem after another,
until you fell asleep on me,
and while you slept,
you would have no more excuses to leave.

But then your friend's friend said something about Alaska,
and then something else about Alaska;
and before I could say anything about the sock I found
that I thought was yours
but wasn't

you were gone.

Meader Pond

I don't remember how much we drank,
I don't remember how much we smoked,
and I don't remember when the mushrooms kicked in;
but I do remember a mountain with a sheer face
looking down at Meader Pond.

I don't remember if I slept,
I don't remember what I ate,
and I don't remember why I cried;
but I do remember being in a little boat
in the middle of Meader Pond.

Van Gogh's brush,
still pining for Mademoiselle Gachet,
paints thick swirls of night over blue.

Halo above the face, edge of aurora flames,
sparks crackle in the treetops,
mountain burning white.

I stared at the stars in the water,
I stared at the water in the sky —
glaciers of light melted into my eyes.

I don't remember how we got to the top of the mountain in the dark
but morning got there at the same time.
I remember standing in an illuminated cloud,
mist weaving among the trees
as the face leaned forward to kiss the pond.

I remember standing on the edge of the face in my untied boots.
The mist cleared and the curve of the wide-open, tree-covered earth
was revealed before me.
I remember the wind telling me I could fly.

Then, I don't remember.

Meditation

I achieved enlightenment.
And the moment it happened I wanted all my issues back.
I felt desperate to be troubled by something.

No angels heralded.
No big handshake congratulations from God.
No sense of peace.
Just an emptiness from where I could see
what I had been missing all along.

In the hereafter of this moment
is just another moment.
What the soul really wants
is to be taken to the circus,
or to make supper and love with you,
breaking bread and breath,
inviting the fire.

As the meditation cushion gets buried beneath our flung-off clothes,
its muffled voice says something like,
"You fool. We were just getting started."

Blind

Miracles happen in reverse,
written right to left.
Desire goes ahead of us.
Not like a reconnaissance mission
but like a kid with a magnifying glass
running out the back door.

We are the woman who can't get pregnant
because she's terrified of becoming like her own lunatic mother,
because history is the story of a trust broken,
of divinity displaced,
of the birth of emptiness,
and how we fed formula to its bright, screaming mouth.

Only when we are naked and dreaming into each other,
upside down in flight
does the memory of another language rise in our throats.
But we swallow hard to keep it from ruining everything,
or we cum and completely forget again.

How could you have known
it was just the beginning?

The Mouse

There is a trash pile in the far corner of a field.
A mouse lives there. The mouse wonders how
the mice on the other side got so big, built that

house with mousetraps in it. The mouse hears
a sound, music of machines. The house is lit
like a tantrum against the darkness.

Welding sparks flash in one of the windows.
Or is that just the TV? The mouse builds a nest
from left-over feathers it finds in a discarded

wooden crate with ANGEL stamped on the side.
The mouse hears another sound, stops and stares
across the field toward the house. An orange

light fills one of the windows, then another.
The mouse's eyes widen as glass breaks and
flames leap up the outside of the house. Soon

the house is engulfed, collapses in on itself,
until there's nothing left but a smoldering pile.
The mouse lifts its nose. Now silent and dark,

the stars and sounds of crickets brighten
like never before. The mouse tucks itself
into the feathers, and closes its eyes.

Dissection

My heart glows like the birth of a new star,
dim and silent.

My belly is a molten world,
still crying.

My legs are the two trees of Eden—
Forsaken and Forgiven—
swinging back and forth,
propelling me across the moment's topography.

My throat is scratched from all the counting.
"No more" it wants to say
but keeps counting.

My eyes are two, mated loons
calling in the dusk
beneath the endless field.

My mouth is a beggar, betrayer,
fucks it all up
and concedes wisdom to the pen.

You are the broken plate that my hands—
Hope and Foolishness—
try to glue back together
want to put bread on and pray over.

My ears are the whippoorwills
that I heard around that one house in childhood,
ignoring my Italian mother's repeated yell
that it's time to come in.

Bound and Lost

Our delicate language
betrayed at the door,
the stars write no poetry
and the earth has already forgotten.

From above, below, and behind
we rode the clouds,
turning our insides out,
chemistry dripping from hair
the smell of wet animals.

Is there a future for us,
or just these earthquakes
and flash floods?

Maybe the calm soil cannot hold us,
and such passion like the blissful child
pouts in defiance of any plan imposed.

Your eyes, the shape of your mouth,
cause my heart to push against my chest
suddenly believing it can fly.

But only tears make it through,
leaving my eyes like newborn rabbits from the burrow,
blindly following the sound of bees
to sun-drenched clover.

Out of Hiding

The water of love rushes into our caves
and flushes us out into the sun, or into the rain,
but to stand there beneath the sky and laugh or cry.

That is my hand you feel on your back,
and that bird over there is my heart
singing about the one thing that never changes.

Pee on the Bee

They put a little picture of a bee
in the urinal.
What for?
So more pee goes down the drain
than on the floor?

Yeah! Pee on the bee!
Pee on the bee!
I get it.

But wait:
I've never peed on a bee before;
no man in his right mind would
unless a lesson in causality,
swiftly and painfully learned,
is what he's aiming for.

So I hesitate,
my retreating turtle in hand,
for what precedent shall be set?
Connecting counter-instinctual wires in the brain
where, one day, I may find myself
showering some previously friendly bumbler
with a rude stream of golden rain.

With unprecedented stage fright,
as if a buzzing from the urinal had begun,
slowly I stuff my whimpering mutt
but then my legs, not waiting, begin to run.

I cannot pee on the bee.
And whose bright idea
or sick joke this was
I wondered as I fled
out the door and into the woods
to find a good ol' tree to pee on instead.

Picking Blueberries at Sturgeon's Cove

As our families arrive,
we pull our cars onto the grassy edge of the driveway
and look up through the windows.
The sky is only cloudy
but the air has that rain-pending feel to it.

Seatbelts click open,
kids bound from their confinements.
We each grab a bucket—five in all—
walk through the tight row of twenty-foot *arborvitaes*
and out onto a long field of tall blueberry bushes
rolling away from us down the hill
toward a calm ocean inlet.

The kids, who are familiar with McCloskey's *Blueberries for Sal*,
start grabbing at blueberries and saying, "*Kerplunk! Kerplunk!*"
as they drop each, deep blue pearl into their buckets.

Being kids, they quickly move on to other adventures.
They all run down toward the water,
except for your daughter, Frances.
She is tucked into the modern papoose behind you,
feasting on every blueberry she can reach.

We talk about what people talk about;
our voices, like the songs of the robins around us,
are a music of friendship.
Slowly we move closer to the water.
Kerplunk! Kerplunk!

The kids are all the way down there, now,
on a little dock they found,
throwing rocks into the tidal muck.
With every *Splat!* or *Splash!*
giggles galore resound into the openness.

The sky takes on a deeper shade of gray
and rain sweeps down on us.
Awestruck children, as if they'd never seen rain before,
cackle and dance on the dock.

Soon, we are soaked and laughing,
licking our lips:
the taste of heaven's wetness
with earth's equally divine blueberries.

The gusts of wind
carry our laughter and excited chatter
down the channel
and out to the barely visible sea.
I imagine
sailors hear the faint Sirens of our joy
and forget their previous courses.
They turn their vessels away
from the wisdom of lighthouses
towards the sound,
the hope of some remembered dream,
and risk being dashed on the rocks.

"Smote His Ruin"

She extended her hand and said —
soft, breathy, almost sexual —

"Thank you."

He was aware of all the fresh soot and oil,
smeared like The Apocalypse
across the topography of his hands.

Mesmerized by the flashing steel in her eyes,
he took her hand lightly and said,

"No problem."

Mouth open, she began to say something,
but stopped, then said,

"I never..."

A sudden commotion erupted outside.
She and he turned to look out the window
to see a little spotted egg leaving a tree,
clenched in the razor maw of a retreating raven,
while several furious, small birds
screamed and attacked.

She and he looked back at each other.
They were still holding hands.

ex

Snow flies in the darkness,
infinity leans on the roof, trusses creak.
To the ghost beside me in my elsewhere bed,
I quietly ask, "What was it you once said?"

That loneliness, that in my worst moments
I spoke through sobs to you about —
the promise I tried to make you responsible for —
is here with me now, unabashed.

Have I ever known love,
or was it just a child's need?

With snowfall piling above,
the ghost whispers an answer. Only now,
in the absence of all that was good about us,
am I able to listen.

The Mystic

for Gary Widger

Somewhere, between the blowing leaves of nothingness
and the hovering black hat of God,
is a wanting mystic,
waiting in the dusk
for the father who never comes.

He stares at the ground,
at an agitated bee
with a severed wing
spinning in the dusty earth.

Some would see it
and stifle with fear
in the coming of all ends.

Some would speak distantly
of God's will,
of the only miracle that could save it,
as their own heel descends.

Fewer still,
certain minds,
would ramble off
into endless dualities.

But only one,
with such detachments of his own,
sees the moment where love is possible,

who picks up the bee that,
in manic rage,
plunges its stinger into the mystic's hand.

But the mystic doesn't flinch.
As the bee's spasms give way to death's stillness,
he says, "I know. I know."

Strawberries in Springtime

Strawberries in springtime:
red earthen jewels
so overpriced and out of season,
so laden with pesticides,
so oddly large from being genetically modified —
so beautiful and inviting.

Maybe we can dip them in chocolate
that came all the way from Peru
on a giant cargo ship that burned enough fossil fuel
to power New York City for a year —
dark, 80% cacao.

I raise the chocolate-covered strawberry to your lips
and you, who without pharmaceuticals
would be locked in a padded room,
smile and take a bite.
Then I take a bite.

We laugh and share a kiss —
stirring all those fears of intimacy
developed in childhood
that will soon tear us apart —
and look deep into each other's eyes,
and share another
strawberry in springtime.

Talking to the Bat

When I was five or six years old,
my father would have a few beers after work
and get his shotgun.
I'd follow him into the dead-end street
in front of our house
at dusk, the time when the bats came out to feed.
The bats would dart all around us,
snatching mosquitoes out of the air.
My father would raise his shotgun
and wait for a bat to cross his sight—

It wouldn't take long before the explosion.
I would cover my ears. The bats would scatter.
On the rare occasion the spray of shot hit a bat,
the bat would be blown to so many pieces
there would be nothing left.

But once, the shot only took off a wing.
The bat fell to the ground in front of me.
I crouched down in the dim light to look at it.
"Don't touch it," my father said. I watched it
try to right itself with its one good wing.

In school, I learned that a bat couldn't see me;
it used radar. But at that age, the only radar
I understood was the kind you see in airplanes:
a green screen with a slow, spinning line.
When something was detected, a little red blip
would appear on the screen. I imagined,
while being so close to the bat, a large
and unusual shape was blipping on its radar.
Maybe its whole screen was red.
Maybe it was all static.

I said to the bat, "Sorry." Then my dad,
using the barrel end of the shotgun,
pushed the bat off the street and into the grass.

He placed the barrel against the twitching,
little body of the bat and pulled the trigger —

the bat disappeared.

Tattle Tale

God does nothing but wait
for the miracle of our own compassion.
The stars are devoid of meaning
but for the math and myth we imagine upon them.
And love? Love is God and the stars:
anonymous, untitled, unfinished.

When I kiss your lips, tea is poured,
a notebook is opened, a pen is picked up,
and the meaning of life,
which is completely up to us to discern,
starts etching across the page.
The words are silent and invisible;
the meaning has to remain secret.
But you know when someone knows it.
There's a wild smirk on their face,
a bona fide shit-eating grin that tells you
they've woken up inside their dream.

Love is God and the stars.

Thanksgiving

Before the snow gets here,
I want to tell you something.
While the leaves are still burning in pre-solstice light,
before our serotonin drops too much
I need your attention.
Before they're heaved and cracked from salt,
hold my hands.
Before the paper gets taped over them,
look into my eyes.
Before we get carried away,
stay.

While we can still leave the door open
and hang out on the front steps,
I'm going to take down the calendar,
unplug the clock
and pretend that I've stopped time.

Come sit with me in the sun
without the family,
all the goddamn food
and the pretense of Christ.
Just one Pilgrim to another,
I want to say, "Thank you."

Signs and Wonders

This would be a waste of time
if not for the child snoring just out of earshot
of his own limbic destitution.

No one would hear this
if not for the way hope keeps changing colors
like a mood ring.

That guru is smiling;
he's commando beneath his robe.
That's why he laughs when someone
mentions God's commandments.

We evolved to have this fight over creation
because some star carelessly thought of water,
because God giggled up the star,
because nothing dreamed of God.

No one would know it,
if someone hadn't jumped
into the passenger seat next to Emptiness
and stuck their head, tongue of history lolling,
out the window going sixty.

Undone

When Abraham awoke from his dream,
where he was about to kill his son
because God told him to,
he looked at the bed next to him—
his son, asleep and safe—
and he felt a deep sense of relief and thought
what a terrible God that would be.

When Noah awoke from his dream,
where God told him to build an ark
and gather all the animals into it, two by two,
because God was going to drown the whole world,
Noah sat there in the dark and listened
to the gentle patter of rain on the roof.
He soon felt only peace and thought
what a terrible God that would be.

When Jesus awoke from his dream,
where he was beaten, nailed to a cross,
stabbed in the side and left to die,
he lay there and listened
to the choir of birds outside,
and he didn't feel forsaken at all.

When I turn on the news
and see abusive parents jailed,
tsunami's swallowing people by the thousands,
and good people killed for their simple beliefs,
I feel God praying to me
to dream only of love.

Vagina

We interrupt this broadcast
for a public service announcement,
brought to you by:

Vagina

A hot bed of influence!
Has made more movies than Michael Cain.

Vagina

Not sold in stores.
Not amassing an army.
Not claiming omnipotence.
But, make no mistake,
it is coming.

Vagina

Unaffected by psychotherapy.
Won't lift a finger, but employs them readily.
Nothing taste quite like it!

Vagina

Can begin and end a war.

Vagina

Can't dial a phone
but it is calling you.

Vagina

No assembly required.
Batteries included.
The Star Gate to another dimension.

Vagina

Unconflicted, yet sometimes pensive.
A really good listener.
Loves that full feeling.
Not just for breakfast anymore!

Vagina

As giving as it is receptive.
A compassionate harbor.
A warm and cozy burrow for a lost and lucky bunny.

Vagina

Act now before it's too late!

We now return you to your regularly scheduled program.

In One Ear

Van Gogh's crows are above me,
speaking their language,
like children plotting
the takeover of an empty barn.

Contrast makes them bright,
pale sky behind the beating black.
And I, the charge of their murder.

Flint of caw upon caw,
throws careless sparks,
and the barn and half the field
go up in flame.

Thick strokes of ink on the page.
This is all I know how to do,
in the hope that certain thoughts
will stop repeating.

I did what I thought I was suppose to do
but, like Vincent in the asylum,
the urge to create put a match to it all,
music of color and line drawing me out.

"Ha Haaa! Ha Haaa!" the crows say
as my paper catches fire.
"You've got another forty years
to get it right."

Vernal Pools

When I was a kid, we had this crazy neighbor
who lived in a big house all by himself.
At Halloween, he wouldn't have a bowl of candy;
he had *buckets* of it.

He would tell us to take as much as we want;
because of that, we believed everything he told us.

One of the things he told us was, "You know
those little pools you come across out in the woods?
Some of them are made by crying gnomes."

He said, "When they feel really sad
about something, they find a low spot in the woods,
sit there and cry and cry and cry. Their tears
fill the space around them and cover them over."

He told us, "The next time you come across
one of those pools, dip your finger in and taste it.
If it tastes salty, then that pool
has a crying gnome at the bottom."

Ever since then,
whenever I find one of those little pools,
I dip my finger in.
I swear, they all taste salty to me.

And whenever I go to the ocean for a swim,
and I get a taste of its salty water in my mouth,
I remember what my neighbor said.
I turn and face the wide, open sea
and stand there in awe,
wondering what the hell could be crying
at the bottom of that.

Walking Home Drunk and Alone

Kitchen stove-hood light
staves off the utter dark,
stares down, wide eyed, at wooden spoons
like the ones mom whacked me with:
illuminated implements of cake and discipline
vibrating with their stirred history.

Rockwellian street wobbles —
am I getting too old for this?

This is what death must feel like:
a ghost trapped in its worst memory of loneliness,
drifting through late shadows;
front porches creak, moan,
shudder and recoil as I shuffle by.

Unity cracked, streetlight-lit leaves
heavy with yolk of incandescence,
darkness and light hang on each other
like swollen, bloody fighters in the fifteenth round.

Now I know why people become homeless,
because all these houses look the same —
the madness of similarities,
because the only thing getting scrubbed around here
is passion and beauty,
like those burnt pots in the sink
that nobody wants to clean anymore.

Cancer fills the abhorrent vacuum —
so put down the vacuum.

The air is chilled out here
but the asphalt is still warm
with a reoccurring dream of sun.
Go ahead. Just lay down. That's right.
Good night.

What It's Not

We are allowed to use everything
because no one is watching.

Which is not to say that God is dead,
just asleep, dreaming
of the kiss of your quiet beauty.

Until then, you can go
smashing and fucking everything in sight.
You can swallow swords, give birth,
maybe, find a giant fissure,
throw a bomb into it
and split the earth in two.

I would recommend, this Christmas,
you skip the feast and the presents,
find a barn, lay naked in the cold hay and cry.

Your family will say that you've lost your mind.
You can smile and say, "That's the whole idea."

Only This Big

We are only this big:
your mothers mixing bowl,
the space within your father's arms,
the bed you grew up in.

We are only this big:
the space between the fences
where the gate was removed
so it would always be open,
home becoming hope.

We are only this big:
the silhouette of leaving,
the fire that stays,
the one who feeds it.

We are only this big:
your hands to your face,
the memory in your eyes
of how you wanted it to be
as big as it actually is.

What Becomes

For all my rebelliousness
against your ideas about safety,
I feel as though I've sold myself
for the greatest one of all.

The more I act out,
the more "mother" you become
because, for you, it's always been
about having all your dolls in a row:
outfits pressed,
hair neatly brushed, braided,
and held together with a colorful assortment
of precious, antique bows.
Not played with, just organized,
like you were.

But all I want to do
is tie all your dolls in a bundle,
strap them on the back of my motorcycle
and ride,
their tiny bows whipping away
in frantic eddies of wind,
trailing behind
as I fly down the back roads.

As summer sun and time burn into dusk,
I switch the headlight on.
I hear your sudden laughter behind me,
feel your hands slide around me,
your arms clasp tight against my chest.

Revelation

What if —
shortly after the end of the world,
when we are all gone
but all our stuff is still here —
some alien anthropologists show up
and the first thing they find
is someone's collection of porn?

They take it all —
and the television, the DVD player,
maybe even the tattered couch
with the big, exploded bloodstain on it —
back to their ship.

After some fancy wiring
to convert their crystal power to 120 volts AC,
they turn on the TV,
put in one of the discs,
sit — cautiously — on the couch,
and push play on the remote.

They will wish they also took the box of tissues
to wipe the tears from their deep bulbous eyes
as they witness the wailing and gnashing of teeth,
as they watch in mute sadness,
just how desperately we tried to be one.

Gainsaid

When I sit on the front steps
and two girls walk by
layered in the final choices of the 20th century,
carelessly stepping on cracks,
I'm convinced more than ever
that this is where earthquakes begin.

I didn't build any of this happiness.
I just bought it
with the generous discount coupons
of my skin color and gender.

Some guy asks me why I'm just sitting here.
I remind him that the Grand Canyon
took millions of years to form. Then I ask him
how he became so eager to put an end to time.

The mailman comes by.
I smile and hold out my hand.
He puts the mail in the mailbox.
"It's the law," he says.

Like I said,
the choices have been made.

Patience

You and I are still here;
there's something we can't forget.

Our internal wars rage towards their ends,
so that they will know the end:
consciousness born of contrast,
how light comes to know itself.

Although we planned it,
we didn't know any of this was going to happen.
Even though we're completely responsible,
it's not our fault.

What we're after out here
is not what we find,
but what we find
is exactly who we are.

When you asked him if you were pretty
and he said, "No,"
you got what you came for.
The exciting backdrop of sex was rolled away,
to reveal the same old brick wall.

But you and I are still here;
we don't seem to be able to forget.

Sometimes, maybe only once,
it actually is for all the right reasons,
but how would we know?
It's never happened to either of us.

So, it'll take some time
before we believe
that we've found what we've been looking for.

Raised by Wolves

for Augusten Burroughs

Your words are a razor
across my wrist
and I can't get enough.

I'm laughing so hard.
Not funny, "Ha! Ha!"
but like the sudden reversal of chemicals
across the synapse,
a choking guffaw blurred by tears.

So much buried anger
wanting to know itself.
My chest is tight.

Like you, I was conditioned
into a state of flinch and cringe,
but this laughter,
like warp drive,
is bending space and time.

I fall through a dazzling wormhole.
Flesh collapses, condenses
into a speck of hydrogen,
primed to burst
into a brand new universe.

At Last

What does the wizard do
when the war is over,
after the coronation and the wedding?

In that place where one story ends
and another begins,
where does the wizard go?

Back to the woods
to walk among the trees,
to sit beside the stream.

There, leaning on his staff
his thoughts whisper
such plain and unmagical things.

Mike Nelson was a founding member of the poetry workshop and performance group, Blood on the Floor. He has frequently presented his work as both an invited reader and an open mic poet at New Hampshire and Maine seacoast readings, including The Black Bean, Busy Bean Café, Beat Night, Café Espresso/Hoot, Café on the Corner, Crackskull, Stone Church and Stone Pigeon. His previous publications include The One in the Middle (2005) and Sometimes at Night (2007). Mike lives in Maine with his son Jay and can be contacted at middle-one@comcast.net.